CW01663982

CARIBBEAN LANGUAGE ARTS PROJECT

Reader

New Places and New Friends

Project Co-ordinator:
Muriel Gill

Co-authors:
Joan Paul
Leonise Serieux-Francois
Julia Hennecart
Gertrude George
Clarita Deterville
Joan Hyacinth
Catherine V. Lewis
Hyacinth Mondesir
Marylene John

MACMILLAN
CARIBBEAN

First published 1987
Reprinted 1989, 1990, 1991, 1992, 1993, 1994, 1995

Published by MACMILLAN EDUCATION LTD
London and Basingstoke
Associated companies and representatives in Accra, Banjul, Cairo, Dar es Salaam, Delhi, Freetown, Gaborone, Harare, Hong Kong, Johannesburg, Kampala, Lagos, Lahore, Lusaka, Mexico City, Nairobi, São Paulo, Tokyo

ISBN 0–333–45151–1

Printed in Hong Kong

Contents

Note to the Teacher

The Readers *New Places and New Friends* and *Story Time Stage 3* are based on the theme 'Our Immediate Community – Our Neighbours'.

To enable the pupil to develop the reading skills listed in the *Teacher's Guide* with ease, the teacher is advised to introduce the chosen theme and story of the Reader as part of the Oral Communication or Social Studies programme. Then, having studied the words listed for the story at the back of the Reader, the teacher should engage the pupil in activities involving word recognition, word attack, spelling and meaning. When the pupil has gained mastery of these concepts and skills, the reading lesson can be introduced. This should be followed up with comprehension exercises, identification of specified words and sentences, and of punctuation marks, and discussion of ideas suggested by the pictures.

Note: do not read for the pupil. Prepare the pupil to read. Let him/her read. Pattern reading for tone and fluency should come after the pupil is able to read the lesson.

Chapter 1

The Greens Move

Peter jumped out of bed.
It was Friday morning.
This was the day the Greens were moving from Fairways to their new home.
'Helen! Helen! It is time to get up. It is Friday. We are moving today.'

'Oh yes, Brother. I am so happy! We are moving to our new home.'

The children dressed quickly and ran to the kitchen.

'Good morning, Mummy. Good morning, Daddy.'

'Good morning, children. You are up early,' said Daddy.

'Good morning, children. Have your breakfast quickly. Then help pack your things,' said Mummy.

'Remember to pack your toys and your books. Put them in this box.'

After breakfast, the children packed their toys and books. They helped Daddy to carry the boxes outside.
'Here comes the truck,' shouted Helen.
'Oh yes, Sister. It is coming.'

The truck stopped by the house. The neighbours came out and helped Mr Green with the furniture.

Mrs Green and the children put the boxes and bags on the truck.

Everyone was on the truck, but Nesto was not there.

'Bow-wow, bow-wow.'
'Where is Nesto?' asked Peter.
'Oh! We forgot him. He is in the yard. Come, Nesto. Jump in quickly. Sit here and be good. We are going to New Gardens. You must come with us.'

'Goodbye,' shouted Peter and Helen.
'Goodbye,' shouted Mr and Mrs Green.
'Goodbye,' shouted back the neighbours.

Everyone was excited as the truck left Fairways.

Chapter 2

Home in New Gardens

'This is New Gardens. Driver, please turn in the first street on the left. Then drive a little way down and turn left into Hibiscus Drive. Stop at the brown and yellow house on your left. It is number thirty-two.'

'Here we are! This is our new home,' said Daddy.
'Oh! What a lovely house,' said Helen. 'I like the colours.'
'Get down, children. We have work to do. Helen, take Nesto with you. Peter, take down the bags and help me carry the boxes. The driver will help Daddy to carry the furniture.'

Mummy and the children carried the boxes and bags into the house.
Daddy and the driver carried in the furniture.
'Thank you, driver. Goodbye!'

The children ran from room to room.
'This is our room. Do you like the colour, Helen?'
'Yes, I like that blue. It is pretty.'
'We'll put our toys and books here.'

Mummy came in to make the beds.
'Will you help me?' asked Mummy.
'I will get the pillows,' said Peter.
'Helen, here is your pillow.'
'No, this is not my pillow. The yellow one is my pillow.'
Helen helped Mummy and soon the room was ready.
'Our room is lovely. Thank you, Mummy. We like it.'
'Let us see the room for Mummy and Daddy.'
'Oh! What a large room. It is not blue like ours. It is yellow. We can help in this one too. We will put up the large bed. It is for Mummy and Daddy,' said Peter.
'Let's put the dresser near the window,' said Mummy.
'May I put the things on the dresser?' asked Helen.
'Yes, you may,' answered Mummy.
'They are in this bag.'
Helen put the things on the dresser.

'That's good! You have worked well. Now let's find Daddy.'
'Daddy! Where are you?'
'I am here. Come and see. Do you like this room?'

'Surprise! A new settee too,' shouted the children.

'I am the first to sit on the settee,' said Helen.

'Everything is in place,' said Mummy. 'Your father has worked well too.'

'Now we are ready to work in the kitchen,' said Helen.
'Is the cupboard clean? Take the things from the shopping basket and put them in the cupboard,' said Mummy. 'Is there soap in the basket?'
'Yes, there is soap,' answered Helen.
'Get the cake of blue soap and put it by the sink,' said Mummy.

'Well, well, we have worked and worked. We have had no time to eat. We are hungry,' said Daddy.
'Oh yes, we have not had time to eat,' said Peter.
'We'll have something to eat, and go back to work,' said Mummy.

'Bow-wow, bow-wow.'
'Oh! Oh! We forgot Nesto.
He is hungry. Give him something too,' said Daddy.

'Put the dishes in the sink, Peter,' said Mummy.
'I will help with the dishes,' said Helen.
'That is very nice of you,' said Mummy, 'but remember to clean the sink.'

'Now our kitchen is clean. You may take some time to play now,' said Mummy.
'It is lovely outside. How nice. We'll go out in the yard,' said Peter.

The children ran into the yard. They were happy to play outside.
'Helen,' shouted Peter, 'there is a mango tree in the yard. Come under the mango tree. Sit by me. What a large yard! We can have a kitchen garden on the left and a flower garden on the right.'

'We will work on that flower garden in the morning,' said Helen. 'We can grow hibiscus, roses and sunflowers. We must get a can to water the garden.'

'When I grow up, I will be a carpenter. I will build a house like this,' said Peter.

'Do you know how to build a house, Peter?'
'Yes, I do. I know I will be a good mason too. Andy's father is a mason and Andy says he'll be a carpenter. I can ask him to help me. A carpenter can paint too.'

'When I have my house, I will decorate it with pretty flowers. I'll buy lovely furniture to put in it. I'll buy a red settee. My flower garden will be on the right and my kitchen garden on the left. It will be a happy home,' said Helen.
'How will you build this house? You didn't say. You are a funny one.'
'Peter, please don't make fun of me. I will not have it. You are the funny one.'

'I am sorry, Sister. I do not want to make fun of you. Andy and I will build your house for you.'

'Thank you, Brother. I am happy now.'

Chapter 3

New Friends

'Oh look, is this the sun?' asked Helen, as she looked out of the window.
'Yes,' said Peter. 'How lovely it looks behind the trees. Our first morning is going to be nice.'

Knock! knock! Mummy walked in.
'Good morning, children. What shall we do today? I must go to the market and to the shop. Helen will come with me. Peter will help Daddy in the yard. Come Helen, we must go. Get a basket for the fruits and vegetables and a bag for the bread.'
'Someone is knocking. Who can it be?'
Peter went to open the door.
'Oh! It's Andy and Rose. Come in!'
Andy and Rose came in and said good day to the Greens.

'We've come to help,' said Andy.
'What can we do?'
'You may come to the shop with us. We need many things.'
'We need sugar, rice, milk, chicken and vegetables.'
'We can get some things from Miss Best. Come on, let's go,' said Rose.
'The shop is near the police station. It is painted blue and white. It's on Poinsettia Street.'
'Look at this, it says "Post Office".'

'Oh yes, it is the Post Office. We get our letters here,' said Rose.
'Do you have a letter to post, Mrs Green?' asked Andy.
'No, not now.'

'On your right is the police station,' said Rose.
'The shop is open. We must cross the street to get there. Look to your right. Look to your left. Look right. Now, let's cross.'

'Good morning, Miss Best,' said everyone.
'Good morning,' answered Miss Best. 'Are you the new neighbours on Hibiscus Drive? Welcome to New Gardens!'
'Thank you, Miss Best,' said Mummy. 'I know we will like it here.'
'Oh yes,' said Helen.

'May I have a box of chicken, some rice, sugar and milk, please?' asked Mummy.
'Yes, you can get the chicken, but I am sorry there's no rice. You can get rice at the next shop.'

Mummy bought chicken, sugar, eggs and milk. She put everything in the basket.
'Thank you, Miss Best and goodbye,' said Mummy.

They all walked out of the shop.
'We must remember to stop at the bakery,' said Mummy. 'We need some bread and cakes.'
'Mm! Mm! I smell cakes and hot bread,' said Helen. 'We must be near the bakery.'
'Here is the bakery, right on Poinsettia Street,' said Rose.
'Come in,' said Mr Frank. 'I have hot bread and nice cakes for new neighbours.'
Mummy bought bread and lots of cakes. She bought a large cake for Daddy and Peter.
'Thank you, Mr Frank.'

'We are home!' shouted the children.
'Come and see,' said Peter. 'We have a surprise for you.'
'Bow-wow, bow-wow.'
'Where is Nesto?' asked Rose.

'Look! Nesto has a home. He has a kennel. A new home for us, a kennel for Nesto.'

Chapter 4

New Gardens

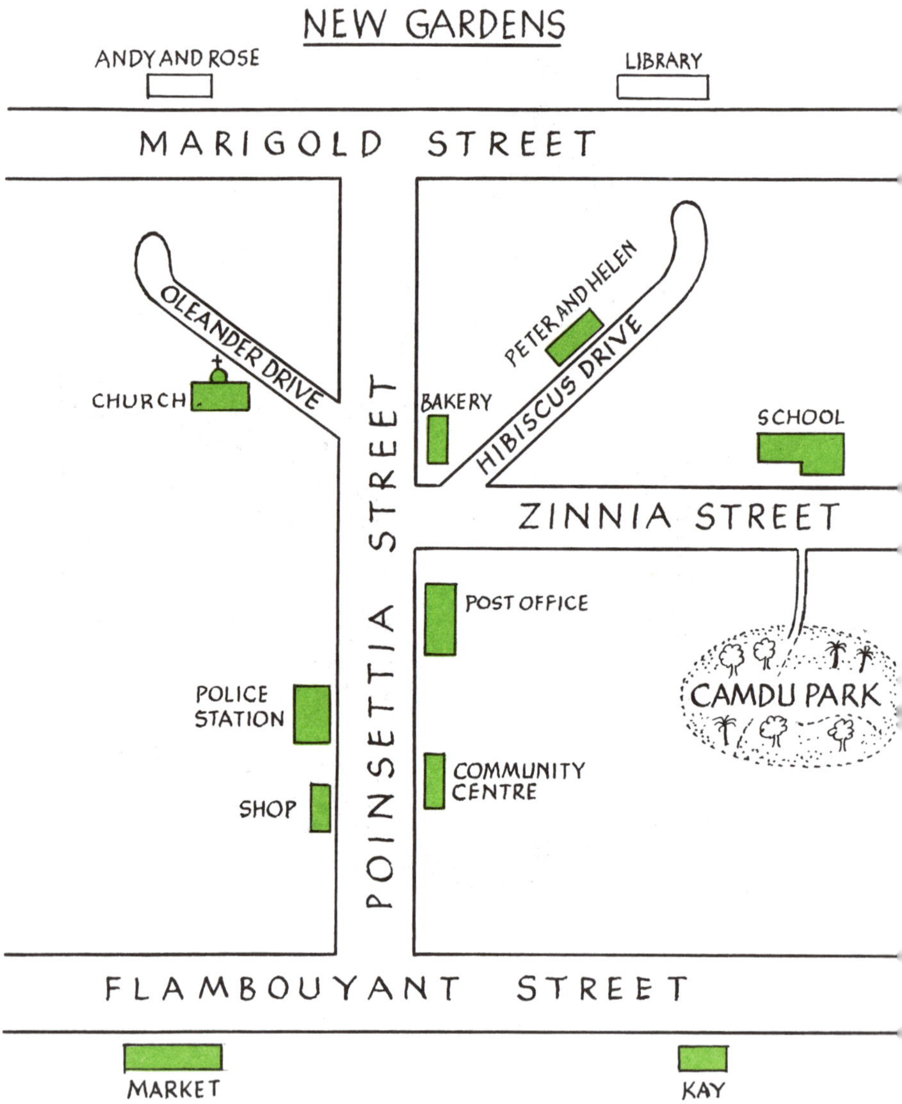

Rose and Andy went with Helen and Peter to find the school on Zinnia Street. This time Nesto went with them. He ran all the way.

'Andy, how did New Gardens get its name?' asked Peter.
'See if you can find out,' said Andy.

They went from street to street.
'Oh!' said Peter. 'I see! Now I know how New Gardens got its name. All the streets have flower names.'
'Andy and Rose live on Marigold Street, and we live on Hibiscus Drive. Miss Best lives on Poinsettia Street,' said Helen.
'You are right. Now let's go on.'

'Look! What is this large picture about?' asked Helen.
'It is not a picture,' answered Andy. 'It tells about a fair at Camdu Park. I forgot to tell you about it. Rose and I will help to decorate the park. We will go to the fair. Do you want to come with us?'

'Yes, we'll ask Mummy. We have worked well, so she may let us go,' said Peter.
'When will it be, Andy?' asked Helen.
'It will be on Sunday at two thirty.'
'We will have lots of fun if we go to the fair.'
They were excited.

The children were surprised to see so many flower gardens in front of the houses. How pretty they looked!
'When we get home we must paint these flowers. We can decorate our room with the pictures.'

'We must not forget to write the names of the flowers,' said Peter. Nesto ran to smell the flowers. 'Come here, Nesto. You must not eat the flowers,' said Helen. 'Let us go back home.'

At home, the children painted the flowers. The first one was the hibiscus. This was the name of the street where the Greens lived. The police station and the shop were on Poinsettia Street. They painted the poinsettia flowers red.

Marigold was the name of the street where Andy and Rose lived. They painted it too. They did not forget the zinnia, for the school was on Zinnia Street.

Kay lived on Flambouyant Street. The market, too, was on this street. They forgot the oleander.

Mother came into the room.
'This is nice work, but where is the oleander? You forgot to paint it.'
'Oh yes,' said Peter, 'that is where we find the church.'
The church was on Oleander Drive.
'I can help you put up the pictures,' said Mummy.
They put up all the pictures.
'How pretty this room looks! Daddy will be pleased to see it.'

Chapter 5

At the Fair

It was raining on Sunday. The children were not happy. They wanted to go to the fair. Helen went to the open window and looked out. She wanted the rain to stop, so she made up this song.

'Rain, rain go away.
The fair is on some time today.
Peter and Helen will not be gay,
If you do not go away.'

Peter came to the window and sang too. They sang many times. Soon the rain stopped. They were happy.

The children got ready and went to the fair with Andy and Rose. The fair was at Camdu Park. Kay was at the fair. The music was gay and sweet. The children sang and danced to the music.

Miss Best was at the fair. She had ice-cream and drinks.
'Let us buy some ice-cream from Miss Best,' said Peter.
'You must buy one for everyone,' said Helen.
Mr Frank was at the fair. He had cakes, bread, chicken and rice.
'We will buy chicken and rice from Mr Frank,' said Andy. 'I like chicken and rice.'
'May we have some, Mr Frank? Thank you.'

Peter and Andy paid to go on the swing. Helen, Rose and Kay went on the swing too. They played in the park. Kay went to hide.
'Where are you, Kay? We cannot find you.'
'Look! Here I am.'
'Oh! She is behind the flambouyant tree.'

'Look! There's Kay's mother. Let's see what she has. Oh, it's a surprise bag.'
Peter paid and got something.
'Ha, ha, ha, what a surprise! It's a green banana.'
Andy got a party hat. He put it on.
'Do you like my brown party hat?' asked Andy.
'It's pretty,' answered Rose and Kay.

Rose and Helen paid to get something from the surprise bag too. Rose got a doll and Helen got an aeroplane. She gave the aeroplane to Peter.

'Come, it's time for us to go,' said Helen.

'Yes, but let's buy some flowers for Mummy,' said Peter.

'There are marigolds, oleanders, zinnias and roses.'

'We will get her some roses and zinnias. She will like them.'

'We must buy something for Daddy too,' said Helen.

'What can we buy?'

'We can buy him some fruits. He likes mangoes and bananas.'

It was a happy day at Camdu Park. What fun everyone had at the fair.

Chapter 6

The Happy Family

The next day Peter and Helen went to the Post Office. Andy and Rose went with them.

'Good morning, Miss Sandy,' said Rose. 'I want you to meet Peter and Helen. They live at number thirty-two Hibiscus Drive.'

'Good morning, children,' said Miss Sandy. 'How are you? I am happy to meet you.'

'We are happy to meet you too.'
'Do you like New Gardens?' asked Miss Sandy.
'Yes, we like it here very much.'
'Are there letters for us, Miss Sandy?' asked Rose.
'I am sorry, there is no letter for you, but there is one for the Greens. Is your name Green?'
'Yes, we are Peter and Helen Green.'
'Well, here is a letter for your father.'

'Thank you,' said Peter. 'We will take it to Daddy.'
The children ran all the way home.

'This letter is from Uncle Mark,' said Daddy. 'He and Aunt May want to come to stay with us.'
'Oh! How nice! Aunt May and Uncle Mark will like it here in New Gardens.'

Peter and Helen were so excited that they got up early next morning.
Helen danced into the kitchen as she sang this little song.

'Who is coming here today?
Uncle Mark and Aunt May.
They have come from far away.
Both of them are here to stay.
Oh, how happy we will be.
Just one happy family.'

Peter came in. He danced and sang with Helen.
They were both very happy.

Uncle Mark and Aunt May came in the afternoon. They drove up in their new car. It had the same number as the old car, 3032. It was a yellow car.

Jan was in the new car. The children were glad to see Jan. She was a bright little girl. She liked to play with Peter and Helen. They both made her laugh and talk.

Uncle Mark took everyone for a drive.
He and Aunt May saw all the beautiful flowers and houses in New Gardens. They loved New Gardens.
'It is a lovely place,' they said.

Before the children went to bed Aunt May said, 'Let us have a play. I will tell you a story and then we will act it.'
Helen did not like acting but she knew she would enjoy the play.

Aunt May told her story:
'Monkey and Donkey lived in the same house. They were both happy.
Donkey did not have to work very hard and Monkey had no work to do.
One day Monkey climbed on to the roof-top and tried to dance. Donkey climbed on to the roof-top and tried to dance too. As he danced, his owner called him down because he was breaking the roof.
Donkey laughed but when he tried to get off the roof, he hurt his back.
The owner was not pleased.
"You are foolish, Donkey. You must not try to do everything that others do." '

'I will play Donkey,' said Peter.
'I'll be Monkey,' said Aunt May.
'Who will be the owner?'
'I will,' said Uncle Mark.
'The table will have to be the roof-top,' said Aunt May.

'You must have some funny clothes to act this funny story,' said Mummy. She got some old clothes for them to put on. They all got dressed.

'Are you ready?' asked Daddy.
'Yes, they are,' replied Helen.
'Then please begin the play.'

Monkey: Look at me, Mr Donkey! Look at me! See how beautifully I can dance upon the roof-top.

Donkey: Yes, it is fun. I can do it too. And I think I'll try it.

Monkey: But you cannot climb. You are too heavy. You will fall and get hurt.

Donkey: Don't be silly. I am not too heavy. I will not fall. If you can do it, so can I. I can do it better. I will not get hurt. How can I?

Monkey: I wish you would change your mind.

Donkey: No! I will not change my mind. You are silly. My mind is made up. Out of my way! Watch me now!

Owner: Oh my! Look at my foolish Donkey! It is trying to dance. You cannot dance.

Donkey: Yes, I can dance. Look at me. I can put up my front legs.

Owner: Get off my roof. You will break it.

Monkey: You silly Donkey. Oh! Your dance is very funny. Please dance again.

Owner: Get off the roof. You will break it. Get down before I knock you off.

Donkey: See how I can jump. You cannot jump like me, Monkey.

Owner: Forget about Monkey. Just get down.

Donkey: Ooof!!!

Owner: Oh my! Donkey has hurt his back.

Monkey: Silly, silly. So silly! Are you very hurt?

Donkey: No, no. Only my back hurts. Oh, oh, oh!

Peter jumped to his feet and laughed.
'Look. I am all right,' he said.
Everyone laughed. It was funny that a donkey could dance.
All the family laughed. It was just one happy family.

Next day Helen and Peter played with Jan and a nice brown doll. The doll could say 'Mammy' when someone turned it over. Helen made a dress for the doll. Jan put a ribbon on its hair.

Peter said the girls had to bathe the doll before they put on her new dress and ribbon. Jan did not want to put her doll in the water.
They made a bed and a settee for the doll. They decorated the doll's room beautifully with shells and flowers.

Mummy and Aunt May were in the kitchen. They talked and talked. They made some guava jelly. Aunt May wanted to take home some jelly. The children had guavas too. Jan put some guavas in a basket to take home.

The next afternoon Uncle Mark was ready to go home. He had helped Daddy with the flowers and vegetables in the garden.
Aunt May and Jan got into the car.
Uncle Mark drove the car.
'We will come to see you again soon,' he said. 'Goodbye.'
'Goodbye,' said everyone.

Chapter 7

School Time

Monday was a school day. Mummy was ready to take Peter and Helen to their new school. They were up early. They got dressed and were soon ready for school.

They were so excited that they did not want to eat breakfast. They only drank their milk and put the bread in their bags for break time.

'Are both of you ready?' asked Mummy.
'Yes we are,' they answered.
Then as they left home for school,
'Bow-wow, bow-wow.'
'Nesto wants to come with us,' said Peter.
'No, no, Nesto, my good dog. You cannot come with us. You must look after our house.'

At school a teacher welcomed them.
'Welcome to our school. You will like it here.'

She took each of them to a class. Peter went to Andy's class and Helen went to Rose's class. Everyone welcomed them.
Soon they made new friends. They each liked their new class, their new friends and their new teacher. They both had very nice teachers.

At school they each painted a picture about the fair. They sang new songs. They played their own music. Helen sang her song about the rain. Everyone liked Helen's song. They played the music to it.

At break time everyone played in the school yard. Soon the teacher came to get them. They were all ready in a line to go to their class.

They did some more work. Then it was time to go home.

As Helen came out, Peter was there to meet her. They had so many things to talk about when they got home. Daddy was glad that they liked their school.
'So you are welcomed here,' he said. 'It's just as if you have lived here a long time.'

After school they helped with the housework. Helen helped Mummy in the kitchen. Peter helped Daddy to get the place ready for the flower garden.
Soon after Rose, Andy and Kay came. They all went out for a walk.

Just outside the police station on Poinsettia Street someone came up to them. It was Kay's teacher. She stopped to talk to them, then went on her way.

The children walked on. Then they stopped near a workshop.
'What is going on in there?' asked Peter.
'Let's just look inside,' answered Kay.

'It's a furniture workshop. See what lovely furniture is made here. Here's a lovely dresser. It looks like Mummy's dresser. I must tell Daddy. If he needs some furniture, he can get it here.'
'You must bring your father to this place,' said Kay.
'Yes, Kay. I'll do that.'

Chapter 8

On the Beach

When Peter got up on Saturday morning, the sun was already up. It was shining brightly and there was no wind blowing.
'How hot it is!' said Helen.
'I wish that we could go to the beach.'
'That's a good idea,' said Peter. 'Let us ask Mummy.'

'Mummy, Mummy, can we go to the beach today?' they asked.
'No, I don't think so,' said Mummy. 'Children who can't say good morning will not go to the beach.'
'Oh! Sorry, Mummy. We forgot.'
'Good morning, Mummy,' said both children.
'May we go to the beach today, please?'

'I think that will be a good idea because it is so very hot,' said Mummy.
'Let's hurry and clean up the house. Then we will go.'
The children helped to clean the house and the yard. They worked hard and soon everywhere was clean.

'You may get ready now,' said Mummy.
The children put on their bathing suits. Helen put the towels in a beach bag. Peter carried the bag as they walked with Mummy to the bus.

Helen and Peter jumped on the big yellow bus. They sat at the front, near the driver. They wanted to see all the places as they drove along. Soon the bus stopped near the beach.
Mummy and the children got off and walked a short way to the beach.

They were surprised to see so many people there. There were people in the water. Some had red, blue and green bathing suits. Others had brown, yellow and white suits.

Some people were sitting on the sand. Many boys and girls were making balls and cakes with the sand.
Mummy found a place under a small tree. She sat on a towel and talked to a friend.

Peter and Helen ran into the cool blue sea.
'Oh, this is lovely,' said Helen. 'The water is so cool, and I feel so good.'

The children splashed in the water, playing water games. Mummy did not want to bathe just then, so she walked along the beach on the wet sand.

While the children were swimming, Mummy watched them.
Then they all went for a walk on the beach. The sun was hot but a cool wind was blowing from the sea.
Mummy joined the children for one last swim and a good splash. The sun was already going down.

They quickly packed their bags. They remembered to put in all the wet bathing suits and towels. The bag was heavy. They walked to the bus. They had had a good time on the beach. Before going to bed, Peter said,
'Mummy, we had a good time today. May we go again next Saturday?'

Chapter 9

The Visitor

'Hurry! It will soon be time to go to the airport.'

'Who is coming today, Peter?' asked Helen.

'Uncle Don, our friend from America.'

'Oh yes, I forgot it was today. I like going to the airport. Let's get ready,' said Helen.

'Children, the car is here to take us to the airport. Hurry.'

The children ran out and soon they were on their way.

'Does Uncle Don live near to Aunt Lea in America?' asked Helen.

'Yes, he is her neighbour. He was our neighbour in Fairways. When he left you were very small.'

'Here is the airport,' shouted Peter. 'I can hear an aeroplane. I like to hear an aeroplane take off — zoom.'

'I can hear it too,' said Helen.
They ran inside and were just in time to see it take off.

‘Oh, look! It’s up in the sky. The pilot is very good. He makes the aeroplane go up and down. I think the passengers like the ride.
There is an air hostess on the plane. The air hostess looks after the passengers.’

'Look! Here comes another! Uncle Don is a passenger on this one,' said Mummy.

'I want to fly in an aeroplane,' said Helen. 'I'll fly right over to America. I'll be an air hostess.'

Uncle Don came down from the plane.

'Uncle Don! Uncle Don!' shouted Peter as he came up to them. 'Let me carry your bag.'

'Welcome to New Gardens,' said Mrs Green.

'Thank you, Mrs Green, I'm happy to be here. How are you, Helen and Peter? You've got so big. You were very small when I left. You look so well. I'm happy to see the two of you.'
'We are glad to have you stay with us. We know you will like it here,' said Peter.

'This is the car. Uncle Don, you can sit in front. Did you enjoy your ride on the plane? I want to be a pilot when I grow up. I'll give Helen a ride.'
'But you want to be a mason, Peter,' said Helen.
'I can be a pilot too.'

'We live on Hibiscus Drive,' said Helen. 'It's not too far from the airport. We'll soon be home.'
'Do you like New Gardens?' asked Uncle Don.
'Yes,' answered the children.

'Do you like America, Uncle Don?'
'Yes, I like America. It's a very big place. It is not as hot as here. It can get very cold. You must visit America some day.'
'Yes, we will,' said Peter.
'You must visit our school and meet some of our friends.'

'We are now on Flambouyant Street. We turn right into Poinsettia Street. The streets all have flower names. This is Hibiscus Drive, where we live. Come in, Uncle Don. Welcome to our new home.'
'What a lovely home you've got. I like it here. I have some presents for you in this box.'
'Thank you,' said Mummy.
'Peter, take Uncle Don to his room.'
Peter carried Uncle Don's bag to his room.
'This is your room, Uncle Don.'
'Thank you, Peter.'

'Come. Let us go outside and see the yard.'
As they went out of the room Mummy opened the box.
'Peter, here is your present.'
'Oh, what a lovely painting-set. And a plane too. Oh! I like them very much,' said Peter.

‘And I have a dresser, some cupboards and a music box for my doll’s house,’ said Helen.

'What do you have, Mummy?' asked Peter.
'I have a very pretty white bag! And see Daddy's watch. It's just lovely.'
'Yes. Daddy will like it.'

Peter took Uncle Don and showed him Nesto's kennel.
'Before I go back I will make a swing for you on the mango tree,' said Uncle Don.
'That will be nice,' replied Peter.
'Then all my friends can come here for a swing.'

Uncle Don had a good holiday. The children liked him. Their friends, Kay, Rose and Andy, came to see Uncle Don. He told them many stories about America and how the people live there. They told him many stories about St Lucia.

Their father, mother and Uncle Don talked a lot about things of long ago. The Greens told Uncle Don how they came to New Gardens. He liked New Gardens. It was a beautiful place with so many flowers.

Uncle Don went to the beach. He visited his friends in Fairways where he and the Greens had lived before. After his holiday Uncle Don went back to America. The Greens gave him some presents. They gave him presents for Aunt Lea too. He promised to write to all of them. Peter and Helen were happy. They knew how to write letters. They promised to write to Uncle Don.

Chapter 10

Mother's Day Surprises

It was Mother's Day. Mrs Green was still in bed. Peter and Helen went to the kitchen and made breakfast. Mrs Green did not know this. Peter got some flowers from the garden and Helen put them in a vase on the breakfast table. They went back to their room to get something. It was a present for Mummy. It was a Mother's Day present.

They placed everything on the table. It was a big surprise for Mummy. They went back to bed.

Soon Mummy came into the kitchen. Before she said anything, Peter and Helen came out and shouted,
'Happy Mother's Day!'

Daddy wanted to know what was going on. He came out to find the lovely surprise.

'Well, well, well,' he said. 'You two have played this game and left me out. I will play a game on you some day.'

The children laughed and laughed. Soon everyone was laughing. Mummy thanked them. 'Now I know that you can help with the breakfast,' she said.

After breakfast, Mummy opened her present. It was a beautiful vase. She liked it. Daddy said, 'You have done everything very well for Mummy. Now I will also do something.' He took out a small box and gave it to Mummy. She was surprised when she opened the box. 'How lovely!' they all shouted. It was a pretty necklace. Mummy was happy and so were they all.

'I want to know if all mothers are as happy as you are,' said Helen.
'Most of them are,' said Peter. 'But some of them have no one to make them happy.'

'How can we help these mothers?' asked Helen.
Mummy said, 'You and Peter can help. Just find out who these mothers are and where they live. I will get something ready for you to take to them.'

Just then Rose and Andy came in. They too had a present for Mrs Green. She thanked them and showed the two presents she had got from her family.
Peter and Helen asked Andy and Rose to name two mothers who had no one to make them happy on Mother's Day.
Mrs Green packed a basket with something for each of them.

The four children went to visit the two mothers. One of them lived near the church. The other lived near Camdu Park.

'Who lives near the church?' asked Peter.

'Everyone calls her ''Mammy'',' replied Rose.

'I don't know if she has any children. We will be her children today. You can call her "Mammy" too.'

They went first to see Mammy.
'Good morning and happy Mother's Day,' they shouted.
How happy Mammy was when she saw the children.

Andy and Rose were already her friends. Now she made friends with Peter and Helen. The children sang to her. She sang to them as well. Her songs were lovely and she sang them sweetly.

Then the children said 'Goodbye, Mammy,' and left.
Mammy shouted, 'Thank you, children, for all the nice things you gave me. Today, I am as happy as any mother.'

They next went to a little house near Camdu Park.
An old woman was sitting outside. She was very pleased to see Andy and Rose. She welcomed their friends, Helen and Peter.
'I am Mrs Peters and this nice boy is Peter. So here we are, friends, and friends we will be.'

Mrs Peters told the Greens that all her children were away and that she lived by herself.
The children gave her the things they had for her. She thanked them. Then she told them a story.
The children liked the story. They told her a story too. She laughed and laughed.
Mrs Peters said, 'You have made me very happy on Mother's Day.'
The children replied, 'That is why we came here.'
They all said, 'Goodbye, Mrs Peters,' and went home.

When they got home, they told their mother all they had done and how the two mothers were happy.
'How nice of you to make others happy on Mother's Day!' said Mummy.

Word List

There are 279 new words in this Reader. The numbers refer to the pages on which the words first appear. The words are also arranged under the chapters of this book.

Chapter 1

1 Peter
jump(ed)
morning
moving
Helen
Fairways
2 our
quickly
kitchen
early
help
your
pack(ed)
remember
books
them
3 after
their
carry
outside
truck
shout(ed)
4 stop(ped)
neighbour(s)
Mr Green
Mrs Green
furniture
everyone
but
Nesto
5 ask(ed)
forgot
yard
6 goodbye
back
excited
as
left

Chapter 2

7 garden(s)
driver
turn
first
street
Hibiscus Drive
number
thirty-two
9 carried
10 ran
room
we'll
11 pillow(s)
soon
ready
large
dresser
let's

near
things
answer(ed)
12 that's
13 surprise
settee
everything
place
14 cupboard
clean
soap
sink
eat
something
15 dishes
nice
17 grow
carpenter
build
18 know
mason
he'll
decorate
I'll
didn't
don't
19 sorry

Chapter 3

20 friend(s)
behind
21 fruits
vegetables
went
open
door
22 we've
need
sugar
rice
chicken
Miss Best
police
station
painted
Poinsettia
Street
24 cross
welcome
there's
25 bought
26 bakery
hot
Mr Frank
lots
27 kennel

Chapter 4

28 Flambouyar
Street
Community
Centre
Zinnia
Street
school
library
Marigold
Street
Oleander
Drive
church
Camdu
Park
29 its
live(s)

30 picture
about
tell(s)
fair
31 when
two thirty
front
32 forget
smell
33 were

Chapter 5

36 made
song
37 gay
if
38 sang
music
sweet
39 ice-cream
40 paid
41 it's
got
42 gave

Chapter 6

43 family
Miss Sandy
meet
44 very
much
45 Uncle Mark
Aunt May
stay
next
far
both
just
46 afternoon
drove
car
same
old
Jan
bright
laugh(ed)
talk
47 took
saw
beautiful
48 before
then
act
knew
would
enjoy
49 told
monkey
donkey
hard
climb(ed)
roof-top
tried
owner
because
breaking
off
foolish
try
other(s)
table
50 clothes
replied
begin
51 beautifully

upon
52 think
heavy
hurt
fall
silly
better
change
mind
53 watch
54 leg(s)
again
57 so
only
58 could
59 Mammy
over
hair
60 bathe
shell(s)
61 guava
jelly

Chapter 7

64 drank
65 each
class
66 own
67 line
more
68 long
housework
69 way
70 workshop
inside

Chapter 8

71 already
shining
brightly
wind
blowing
idea
72 hurry
everywhere
73 bathing
suits
towels
bus
along
short
people
white
74 found
small
cool
feel
75 splash(ed)
games
76 while
swimming
last

Chapter 9

77 visitor
airport
Uncle
Don
America
Aunt Lea
hear
79 sky
pilot
passenger(s
ride

air hostess
plane
80 another
82 I'm
84 cold
visit
you've
present(s)
88 holiday
St Lucia
89 ago

Chapter 10

91 still
vase
94 done
also
95 most
96 show(ed)
99 woman
100 away
herself
why